Learn the game!

YO-YO

Licensed exclusively to Top That Publishing Ltd
Tide Mill Way, Woodbridge, Suffolk, IP12 1AP, UK
www.topthatpublishing.com
Copyright © 2014 Tide Mill Media
All rights reserved
0 2 4 6 8 9 7 5 3 1
Printed and bound in China

INTRODUCTION

Have you ever tried a yo-yo and never got past doing the basic throw and catch?

Have you ever wanted to impress your friends with lots of cool yo-yo tricks?

Have you ever wondered how yo-yos work and how they became so popular?

If you have answered 'yes' to any of these questions, then this book is ideal for YOU! All you need is a yo-yo! Buy one (or even two) from a toy shop and you are ready to yo-yo-a-go-go!

This book will take you on a whirlwind journey through all things 'yo-yo' related! During this journey you will learn how to do many tricks with one and two yo-yos. You will also become very brainy about how the yo-yo works, so you can impress all your friends!

Are you sitting comfortably? Well you shouldn't be!

Get up and grab the nearest yo-yo, flex your fingers and you are ready to start.

YO-YO UPS AND DOWNS

The ancient Greeks were the first yo-yo people. They are known to have used the yo-yo as early as 2,500 years ago! This makes the yo-yo the second oldest toy in history (the oldest is the doll).

'Emigrette'

The yo-yo became very popular in 18th-century France (where it was known as an 'emigrette'), and also in places as distant as Malaysia, Persia and the Philippines.

Crowd Pleaser

A young man called Pedro Flores emigrated from the Philippines to America in 1920. He soon realised that no one in his new town had ever seen a yo-yo before! When Pedro practised his tricks during his work breaks, large crowds of people would watch him.

Realising the crowd's fascination with his yo-yo tricks, he began making 'Flores yo-yos'! The word yo-yo in his native Philippine language means 'come, come'.

Mr Yo-Yo

A few years later, the Flores yo-yo was spotted by the man we now know as 'Mr Yo-Yo' – Donald F. Duncan! Donald bought Flores' business and played a huge part in making the yo-yo the huge success that it is today.

Out of this World

The yo-yo has literally been 'around the world'! On 12th April, 1985, NASA took the first yo-yo into space on the Space Shuttle *Discovery,* in order to do some tests on how it was affected by gravity (or lack of gravity)!

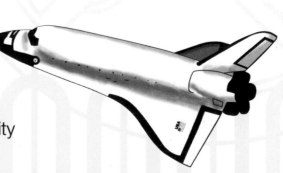

THE BASICS

Time to start with some basic pointers. Boring as these tips may be, until you know about the correct string length, how to create a slip knot, how to wind up a yo-yo and how to stay danger free, you will not make much progress at all!

String Length

The string should be about the length from your belly button to the floor. If you need to cut the string, remember to leave 7 cm extra at the top as you will need to make your first loop and slip knot!

Of course, you might decide that you like a slightly longer string, as it all comes down to your own preference!

SLIP KNOTS

This is the knot which should be used to attach the yo-yo string to the middle finger of your best hand.

1. First of all, you have to make a loop (most yo-yos come with this loop already).

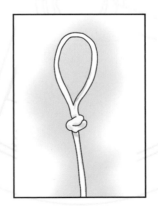
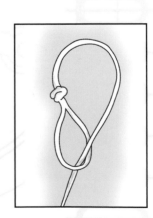

2. Push the string a little through the first loop, so that you have another loop. This is where your finger goes.

Customise

You will notice that the first loop by itself will be way too slack. It is meant to be this way, so you can use a slip knot to customise the string to your exact finger size. It's all very clever!

1. When the yo-yo is at the end of the string (not the end of your finger), grab one of the yo-yo discs and place your finger over the groove that separates the two discs.

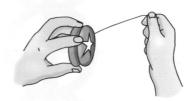

2. Wrap the string once round the yo-yo and over your finger.

3. On the second and third times round, wrap the string round the yo-yo and underneath the finger.

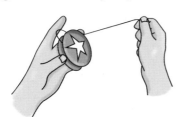

4. Remove your finger and keep winding up (not too tight).

5. As you reach the top, wrap the string a bit tighter.

6. Finally, when the yo-yo is wound up, do one basic throw and catch to try out the string.

Play It Safe

Playing with a yo-yo can be a dangerous activity (mainly to people watching), so please make sure that you have enough room around you to throw the yo-yo in any direction – 2 metres all around you should be enough.

You should not practise too near a glass window, priceless furniture or, even worse, other people who you could hit! You should also be wary that the yo-yo doesn't hit you at a great speed, so concentrate and stay careful!

THROW AND CATCH

This is the first trick you should learn – and it is the first one that most people think of when they pick up a yo-yo!

1. Wind the yo-yo up. Your palm should be facing upwards with the yo-yo on it.

2. When you are ready, throw the yo-yo forward and down over the edge of your fingers.

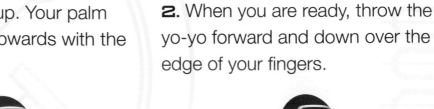

3. Once the yo-yo has left your hand, turn your palm over to face the floor and prepare for the catch.

4. As the yo-yo hits the bottom of the string, pull the yo-yo up using a sharp wrist movement. It should return to your hand, where you have the choice of catching it, repeating the same move or doing some tricks!

THROWING A 'SLEEPER'

A sleeping yo-yo is when it spins at the end of the string. Practise this trick well as it is used in most of the tricks that are written in this book!

1. Start in exactly the same way as the basic throw and catch, but as the yo-yo reaches the end of the string, try to soften the impact.

2. If you can do this properly, the yo-yo will stay at the end of the string.

3. Let the yo-yo spin for a few seconds and then, with a sharp flick up of the wrist, send the yo-yo back up the string to catch it again.

4. Try to see how long you can make the yo-yo 'sleep' and still successfully return it to the hand.

FORWARD PASS

This trick is used to start many moves, so take your time to learn it properly!

1. Move your arm backwards but out to the side. The palm should be facing upwards.

1.

2. Bring your arm forwards in front of you – as if you are about to release a tenpin bowling ball using a backhand spin!

2.

3. At the point when you would release the 'bowling ball', release the yo-yo.

3.

4. The yo-yo will roll off your fingers and fly straight ahead, and then return to your hand which should be facing palm upwards.

4.

WALK THE DOG

It's time to exercise your pet yo-yo!

1. Throw a fast sleeper.

2. Lower the yo-yo gently onto the floor.

3. Now simply walk along behind the yo-yo as it rolls by itself along the floor (as if you are taking a dog for a walk)!

4. A sharp tug on the 'lead' will return the dog to you!

5. If you can whistle, or summon your dog back, this will make your audience laugh!

AROUND THE WORLD

Make the yo-yo do a full circle! When you have learned the sleeper and forward pass, you can combine both tricks with this move.

1. Throw a 'sleeper forward pass'. This is when you throw the yo-yo forward (as described in the forward pass) and make it stay spinning at the end of the string.

2. Move your arm in a circle past your head and over your shoulder in a backwards direction to complete a full circle. The yo-yo will follow, remaining asleep at the end of the string.

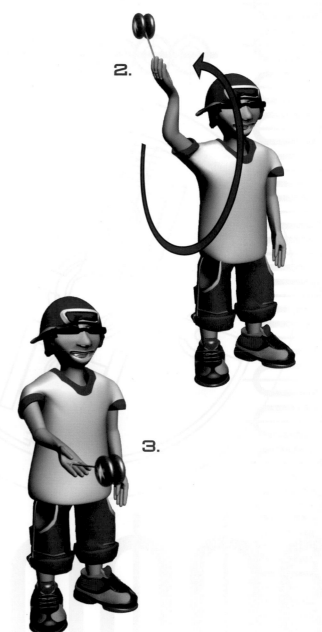

3. Once a full circle has been completed, give a quick tug on the string to pull the yo-yo back into your hand which should be facing palm upwards.

HOP THE FENCE

This neat trick looks great but is not too difficult.

1. Throw the yo-yo downwards (it doesn't have to sleep).

2. Instead of catching the yo-yo as it comes back up the string, let it flip over your wrist so it can go down once again.

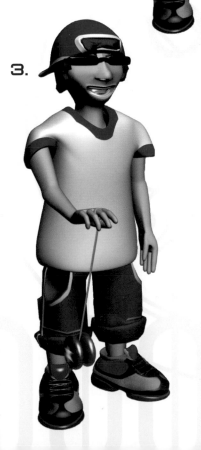

3. You can repeat this trick again and again, but be warned, depending on the hand the yo-yo is in, the string will either gradually get looser or tighter!

OVER THE SHOULDER

1. Throw a sleeper.

TOP TIP!

If you're still a bit shaky when you throw a sleeper, try distracting people by talking them through the trick.

2. Raise your hand to about ear height and put your elbow in front of the string.

3. Drop your hand down and jerk the string so that the yo-yo wakes up from its sleep. It will then follow the string back up over your shoulder and into your hand.

LOOP THE LOOP

This trick looks good with one or two yo-yos!

1. Make a forward pass.

2. When the yo-yo comes back, don't catch it.

3. Instead, direct it over your wrist and then back out again repeating the forward pass. This will make it loop.

4. Once again, depending on which hand you use, you either tighten or loosen the string with each repeated move!

Take time to learn this trick as it will come in handy later on with other tricks! Try to get it right once, twice and then three times in a row. Keep practising to see how many you can do. Your arm shouldn't move much at all, as all the action should be in your wrist.

Reverse Loop the Loop
This is where you send the yo-yo in the opposite direction with a loop the loop. It's much harder than you may think!

SPAGHETTI

Make the delicious string disappear!

1. Throw a sleeper.

2. Using your free hand, grab the string about halfway down.

3. Now swing your yo-yo hand down and gather up the string using both hands.

4. Hold the spaghetti bunches near your mouth when you have collected plenty.

5. As you let go of the string, make a loud slurping noise and the string will look as if it has disappeared into your mouth!

6. Return the yo-yo to your hand, then rub your stomach and tell the audience how good it tasted!

BREAKAWAY

This is the starting move for many advanced tricks. The aim is to throw the yo-yo out (not down) on the release. The yo-yo should move from shoulder height on one side of your body to shoulder height on the other side.

1. Begin with your elbow at shoulder level and pointing outwards (just as if you were flexing your muscles).

2. Release the yo-yo and bring your elbow down sharply towards the ground.

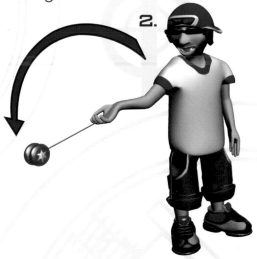

3. The yo-yo should fly outwards and down and begin to sleep.

4. At this point, swing your arm across the front of your body (like a pendulum) and towards your other shoulder.

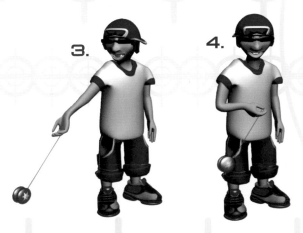

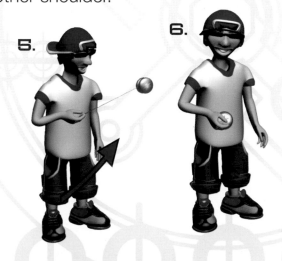

5. The yo-yo will, of course, follow your arm, but first it will pause for a second, which is why the move is called 'breakaway'!

6. Bring the yo-yo back to your hand to end this trick.

THREE-LEAF CLOVER

This is a multiple loop the loop move.

1. Start with a skyward loop the loop.

1.

2. Use your wrist to redirect the yo-yo back out in a straight ahead loop the loop.

2.

3. Finish with one downward loop the loop, and return the yo-yo to your hand once again. You do not catch the yo-yo until the trick is finished (it is all in the wrist).

3.

TOP TIP!
If your yo-yo wants to sleep every time you throw it out, this means that your loop is way too loose around the axle and needs to be tightened.

PINWHEEL

This is a move which involves a breakaway and mini around the world combination.

1. Start with a breakaway, for example, flexing your muscle and throwing a sleeper out to your side.

2. Swing the yo-yo in front of you across your body.

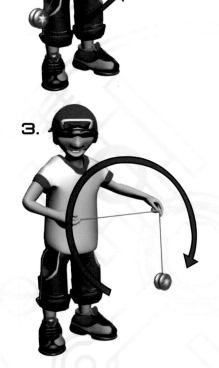

3. As the yo-yo comes up to the other side of your body, grab the string about halfway up with your free hand and do a couple of mini around the worlds (either clockwise or anticlockwise).

4. Release the string and this should cause the yo-yo to return safely to your hand! If this doesn't work, then try jerking your wrist a little once you have released the string.

CHOOSE A NEW YO-YO

You will soon be reaching the two-yo-yo tricks section, so you will need to make sure you have more than one yo-yo! It's time to buy a shiny new yo-yo if you don't already have a spare. Here are some different types of yo-yo for you to choose for your two-yo-yo tricks.

Non-sleeping Yo-Yo
(fixed string and fixed axle)

This yo-yo can only perform about six basic tricks, because when the yo-yo hits the bottom of the string, it immediately returns to your hand. This means that it cannot 'sleep' at the bottom of the string.

Fixed Axle/Slip-string Yo-Yo

The middle (axle) is fixed to (and spins with) the yo-yo. The fixed axle spins in the loop of string while it sleeps. Working with this yo-yo gives you a good training for the basic tricks.

Trans-axle and Ball Bearing Yo-Yo

This has a plastic sleeve or ball bearing that basically rotates independently from the two halves of the yo-yo. It can therefore 'sleep' for a lot longer than a fixed axle yo-yo, which opens up a whole world full of tricks for you to try to master!

Clutch and Brake Yo-Yo

The yo-yo with a brain! It is easy for this yo-yo to 'sleep', as the amazing clutch returns the yo-yo to your hand as soon as it starts to slow down!

As well as all of these yo-yos, you can also get ones that light up as you play with them, and even yo-yos that play tunes!

Yo-yos are fairly inexpensive, so you may be able to choose a few different ones to add to your collection.

TWO-YO-YO TRICKS

Here are a few helpful hints and tips.

If you can do all of the tricks so far, then you are ready to think about moving on to two-yo-yo tricks. It will help if you have two yo-yos that are similar when you practise these tricks (i.e. two of the same type).

It is important for you to practise with both hands individually – especially with your weaker hand – in order to make sure that each trick will work!

Many of the tricks featured in this book so far can be done with two yo-yos at the same time. Don't be afraid to experiment and let your imagination run wild. You can even try doing two different tricks at the same time!

WALK THE DOGGIES

1. First of all practise the 'Walk the Dog' trick shown on page 9.

2. Experiment with setting one yo-yo dog down on the ground a little before the other yo-yo dog.

3. Try letting the doggies go off in slightly different directions!

4. Act as if you are being pulled apart and don't know which dog to follow!

DOUBLE BREAKAWAY

1. Practise the 'Breakaway' trick found on page 15.

2. One hand needs to be further out from the body so that the two yo-yos don't collide!

3. The hardest part is trying to catch both yo-yos at the end of the trick!

TWO LOOP THE LOOPS

1. Practise the loop the loop and reverse loop the loop tricks with each hand individually before you attempt both hands at the same time!

2. The idea is that one hand will loop the loop, and the other hand will 'reverse loop the loop'.

3. You can try making both yo-yos go in the same direction.

4. Time it so the yo-yos are synchronised with each other. Then make the yo-yos go at different times.

HOW DO YO-YOS WORK?

The movement of your yo-yo is simple (up, down, round and round), but the concepts behind the basic yo-yo are not so simple!

There are many physics concepts that can be applied to the art of yo-yoing.

The main theory is called Newton's Second Law of Thermodynamics. This is all about conserving energy.

When a yo-yo leaves your hand, the energy has to go somewhere. It can either go into the up-and-down motion (translational), into the round and round motion (rotational) or it can be lost to friction against air and the string.

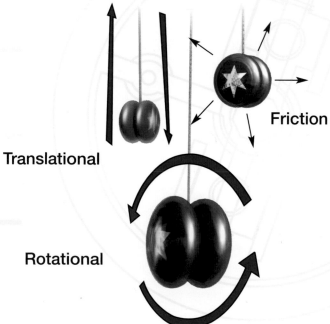

Translational

Friction

Rotational

Gravity pulls the yo-yo downwards when it leaves your hand. As the string is wrapped around the yo-yo and attached to your finger, the yo-yo has to rotate as it drops.

HOW DO YO-YOS WORK?

When the yo-yo reaches the bottom of the string, it can't drop any further. If left like this, the friction between the axle and the string will eventually get rid of the rotational energy, and the yo-yo will come to a rest.

Before this happens, you can of course give a tug of the string to send the yo-yo back up to your hand. This causes friction on the string and axle to increase so that the axle does not slip within the string, which in turn causes the yo-yo to climb the string once again.

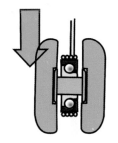 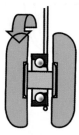 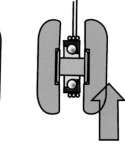

Next time you do a simple throw and catch with your yo-yo, just think about how this is achieved.

Downwards   **Rotating**   **Upwards**

PUT ON A SHOW

If you get really good at all the tricks you have read about, then you may feel you are ready to perform in front of an audience.

You've probably already shown off your tricks to family and friends, but if there is a local talent contest, or even a fun day that requires some entertainers, then you could offer to take part and show people how wonderful you are!

The more you perform, the better you get, so keep practising and keep performing!

WORLDWIDE

Every year, there are juggling conventions and competitions held all over the world.

Many of these conventions are a great place for yo-yo tricksters to turn up, swap tricks and make new friends. Ask an adult to help you search for suitable websites as the internet is a good place to find information about such events.

If you cannot find a convention near you, then perhaps you could try to organise your own yo-yo competition and see who is prepared to travel to your home town to get involved!

STARTING A CLUB

If you can teach someone to use the yo-yo, and then the two of you teach another two people, you will soon have enough people to form a yo-yo club.

Your club could take on the formality of hiring a venue (perhaps an adult can help you with organising this), or you could simply arrange that during one lunch hour at school every week you and your friends will bring in your yo-yos and swap tricks with each other. These activities will soon attract more people to join your club!

WHAT NEXT?

If you've enjoyed perfecting the tricks in this book, why not try making up some of your own?

Keep yo-yoing!!!!